a
JOURNEY
in the
RIGHT
DIRECTION

thoughts on discipleship for youth

ISBN 978-1-56344-714-3

Gustavo Crocker, Ed Belzer, Clive Burrows, Tim Evans, Jayme Himmelwright, Kyle Himmelwright, Todd Waggoner and Sabine Wielk.

introduction

Christianity. Holiness. Ministry. There are some common questions about these themes that many of us have asked, and have been asked by others. A few of us sat down to reflect on these questions, and as is usually the case, we ended up with even more questions of our own. We wrote those down too, so that together with you, we can embark on a journey.

What you're holding in your hand is only the beginning. These are a few questions and the beginning of answers. They are not meant to be complete nor comprehensive. They're really just to start you thinking. And together with others who are on this journey, and with God's help, we would like to discover more answers.

There is no prescribed way to use this material, but it will probably work best if you explore the questions and answers with people around you. Whether you do that sitting on benches in a church or around a table in your favourite café is up to you. All we ask is that you honestly seek answers beyond the ones given, and that you don't stop asking these, and other, questions.

We also ask you to help us develop this material. If you'd like to turn it into a script and record a video, host a quiz-show, draw a comic or give us your thoughts in a written form, we would love to hear from you. With your permission, we'd also like to make your contributions available to others. Please email your thoughts, comments and ideas to be shared with the rest of us to journey@eurasiaregion.org – for updates from others you might want to check www.eurasianazarene.org ("resources" link).

May God give us the courage and perseverance to ask the difficult questions throughout our journey, and the openness to go where that will take us.

Your Fellow Travellers,
Clive, Ed, Jayme, Kyle, Sabine, Tim & Todd

P.S. If you received this in English and English is not your preferred language, please check with us to see if translations into your language are already being produced. You can also download free copies of this book to print or share with others.

a JOURNEY in the RIGHT DIRECTION

chapter one

CHRISTIANITY: THE BIG PICTURE

by Jayme Himmelwright

1.1 What God Is Like

Q: I have heard God described in so many ways (loving, judging, everywhere, in heaven, watching, in action). So what is God really like?

God is love. The very fibers of who God is are love. Let me explain. Okay, we are going to get a little deep here for a minute. In order to love, you have to have someone to love, right? Within God, we find three persons (the Father, the Son and the Holy Spirit) who love one another (John 17). God is a circle of love. That means that the very person of God embodies love. However, God's love is not self-centered. That is why He could not be satisfied with just keeping His love for Himself. Instead, God's love is always moving out from Him to love others. That is why He created us. He created us in order to love us. In His love, God is always seeking a relationship with us.

God is so great that we could never truly define Him with our limited understanding and language. However, love encompasses all of His traits. This love is what sets God apart from all else and makes Him holy. We must remember that this is not an overly-emotional, sentimental type of love. This is a love that requires self-denial and discipline. It is a love that is truth (Romans 12:9).

Discussion Questions

1. How do you perceive God?

2. Do you understand Him in only one way (for example, only as a judge), or can you see His many dimensions?

3. Do you know God as love? How can you come to know God more fully?

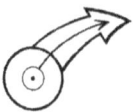

1.2 The Story the Bible Tells

Q: I have read parts of my Bible and I do not see the connection between the Old Testament prophets and the New Testament gospels, or the Psalms of David and the letters of Paul.

The Bible is God's love story. God has been working to bring about perfect relationship in His creation since the beginning of time. God had a relationship with Adam and Eve, but they broke that relationship with Him, and the broken relationship continued for generations. Then, God chose Abraham's family, the Israelites, to be His special people. God did not do this because He only loved them and because He had given up on the rest of the world. Instead, He gave the Israelites a special responsibility. They were to show the rest of the world who God was so that the other nations and peoples would also come to be in relationship with Him (Genesis 12:2-3; Exodus 19:5b-6). However, the Israelites did not do such a good job. They drifted away from God, so God let them have kings to guide them (1 Kings 8:41-43; Psalms 67:1-4). They still turned their backs on God, so God sent prophets to warn them, but they did not listen (Isaiah 2:2-4; Isaiah 66:18-21; Jeremiah 1:5).

Then, God did the most loving thing possible (John 3:16; 1 John 4:9-12). He came to Earth as a human to restore the relationship between God and humanity. Jesus gifted the world with two important things to take His place when He left. Firstly, He gave the Holy Spirit—God's presence with us every day—to help us be in right relationship with God. Secondly, He established the church. The church is now the people of God. We have been given the special responsibility to show the world God, so that they can be in relationship with Him (Matthew 28:18-20; Acts 1:8).

The rest of the New Testament is the story of how more and more people came into right relationship with God as the church grew. Finally, in Revelation, we have a picture of what will one day be—all nations gathered together before God—the fulfillment of God's love (Revelation 5:9-10, 7:9-10). So you see, the Bible is one continuous story of God's loving pursuit of all people.

Discussion Questions

1. How can you relate the perspectives that we get of God in the Old Testament to the perspectives that we get of God in the New Testament?

2. Does our belief that Jesus came to reveal God more fully add another perspective?

1.3 The Role That Jesus Plays

Q: I understand that Jesus died for my sins, but is that the whole reason for Jesus coming to the earth?

Jesus was both completely God and completely human. (Don't worry. You don't have to fully understand that. It is a mystery that we believe.) Therefore, Jesus revealed both God and humanity to us.

Firstly, Jesus showed us who God really is (Luke 10:22; John 14:9; John 17:6). For the first time in history, humanity was able to see God in a concrete, physical way. We were able to more fully know Him, love Him and be in relationship with Him.

Secondly, Jesus showed us what humanity was meant to be. Genesis 1:26 says that we were made in the image of God. That means we are able to be in relationship with God and in relationship with others. Jesus showed us and taught us what it is like to be in perfect relationship with God and to live in selfless, loving relationships with others (Mark 12:29-31). He showed us how to use power and resources selflessly. Jesus showed us what we will someday be like. He painted a picture of how we will be in eternity and taught us how to live in the present (John 17).

Finally, God did not abandon us when Jesus ascended into heaven. Instead, God, the Holy Spirit, remained with us to empower us to live in right relationship with God and with others (John 14:15-20).

"And I pray that you, being rooted and established in love, may have power, together with all the saints, to grasp how wide and long and high and deep is the love of Christ, and to know this love that surpasses knowledge—that you may be filled to the measure of all the fullness of God" (Ephesians 3:17-19).

Discussion Questions

1. What do we learn from Jesus about God?

2. What do we learn from Jesus about what humanity is meant be?

1.4 What Happens In The End

Q: I have friends that are good but not Christians. I don't understand how God punishes them but not the mean Christians from church I know. Is there hope for them?

This is a difficult question. Honestly, I think that only God knows the answer. We can see both sides. God is loving and merciful, yet He is also just. "The Lord is slow to anger, abounding in love and forgiving sin and rebellion. Yet he does not leave the guilty unpunished" (Numbers 14:18).

God is just. There are many parables and teachings that tell of future judgment. Many Scriptures state that few will enter heaven (Matthew 7:13-14, 1 Peter 4:18). The Bible also tells us that Jesus is the only way to the Father (John 14:5-6; Acts 4:12).

On the other hand, God is love. Will God show mercy? Will He look at the motives of the heart? Will His justice take into consideration the circumstances (Romans 2:12-16)? The Bible does tell us "that at the name of Jesus every knee should bow, in heaven and on earth and under the earth, and every tongue confess that Jesus Christ is Lord, to the glory of God the Father" (Philippians 2:10-11). I do not think that we can put God "in a box" and limit what He can and will do. God is the ultimate judge, and He is a God of hope.

What we know for sure is that through Jesus we are saved (John 3:16). In this life, we must live for God and share Him with others. God, in His wisdom, will know what to do with those who have not accepted Him when the time comes.

Discussion Questions

1. Do we have to fully understand everything about God?

2. How can we live with mystery?

chapter two

CHRISTIANITY: THE PURPOSE OF THE CHURCH

by Ed Belzer

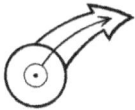

2.1 Being A Family

Q: There are some people in my church that drive me crazy. Do I really have to go to church and be around them?

Yes. Next question?

Just kidding! Actually, we were created to have a relationship with each other, and God wants to have relationship with us. Relationships, however, are very difficult. Just take a look at our world: there is conflict all over the globe. And sometimes this conflict happens in the church, to the extent that there are people in our church that drive us crazy. You are not alone. This is a really good question that we need to wrestle with.

Let's go back to the context of the great commandment that Jesus gave us in Matthew 22:34-40. For us, becoming and doing what God calls us to be and do, can only happen when we love God with all of our heart, soul and mind. Once we begin to love God in this way, then we begin to have the ability to truly love what God loves: people.

As I deal with people that drive me crazy, I think about the fact that God created every one of us in God's image (Genesis 1:26). So every person, regardless of their appearance, their perspective, their attitude, their behaviors, their temperament or whatever, was created by God. He or she is loved by God so much that He was willing to die for them. I have to remember this in order to begin dealing with the people who drive me crazy in my church.

We are commanded to love everyone; however, this doesn't mean that we have to be best friends with everyone. It does mean that we have to do our best to live "at peace" with those in the church.

Check out chapter 4 of Ephesians. In this chapter, Paul gives us some great ideas to help us deal with people in the church. There have been many times when I have had to go to this chapter and pray it into my life again and again. Verse 2 really speaks to us regarding our relationships with others. I came to this realization: I knew it would be work to be around people who aren't Christians (you know, the whole idea that sinful people do sinful things). So I know that it will be work, that it will take a lot of patience and love to be around non-church kinds of people. But I had this idea that it would be easier to be around people in the church.

But then in verse 3, Paul's words confronted me on this issue: "Make every effort to keep the unity of the Spirit through the bond of peace." He says that it was going to take some effort, it was going to take work, and it wouldn't necessarily be easy to get along with others.

Sometimes it is hardest to be around people we love the most, because we know them so well. We know their weaknesses, we know who they are, and the reality is that every one of us has issues in our lives that tend to annoy others.

There are people in my family that drive me crazy, but they are still my family. The Church is the body of Christ, the "family of God." We must do everything we can to live at peace with everyone.

Discussion Questions

1. Who are the people who drive you crazy, and why do they drive you crazy?

2. What "image of God" do you see in their lives?

3. What is one thing about those people that you can appreciate?

4. In what ways can you pray for those people?

5. What are things about yourself that might drive other people crazy?

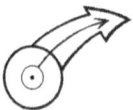

2.2 Distributing Grace

Q: Jesus seems to hang out with and forgive some of the worst and overlooked people. How can the church become more like Jesus?

You are absolutely right in that Jesus came and hung out with the worst and overlooked people on Earth. We read about Jesus doing this in the story of Zacchaeus in Luke 19:1-10. Jesus knew that people were "muttering" about Him hanging out with "sinners." And Jesus told them, "The Son of Man came to seek and to save what was lost."

We have to remember that one of the purposes of the church is to reach out to those that don't know Jesus! It is easy for the church to become just a safe place where its members can hide and stay safe. However, we have to deal with some realities.

If you as a Christian hang out with "sinful" people, one will influence the other. Either you will draw them towards Christ or they will draw you away from Christ. Are you strong enough to influence others towards Christ or will they influence you away?

When I was a teenager, I could not have spent time in the bars around alcohol. I was not strong enough to deal with the temptations that it would bring. Today, alcohol has no temptation for me, and to be around it doesn't influence me at all. In fact, I feel compassion for the people whose lives are controlled by this substance.

In the church, we have a huge challenge: to reach people for Christ and then help them grow in the faith.

Many churches are good at reaching out to people, but then they struggle with discipling them. But we are not just about seeing someone "get saved." We also know that there is a lifetime of learning and growing in our faith. It can seem more exciting to be reaching new people for Christ, but we want to see people grow and keep their faith until they go to Heaven.

In Acts, we read the account of the early church. Luke reports that 3,000 were added to the church in one day. He records later that they met together every day to break bread, pray and go over the apostles' teachings (Acts 2:42). We need to be grounded in faith in Jesus Christ; then we can hang out with people who desperately need Jesus.

The reality is that the church has people at every level of spirituality. Some are just checking out what it means to be a Christian; some have just accepted Christ, some are growing in their faith, and some are deeply committed, knowledgeable Christians whom we would consider to be mature. We should be continually reaching new people, and then help them grow in their faith.

There are many ways in which we can exercise our faith and reach out to people as a church. One idea is to volunteer as a church or youth group in a soup kitchen to feed homeless people. I heard the story of one youth group that raised money every month to provide an apartment for women trying to get away from prostitution. It could even be as simple as joining that person who is always sitting alone at lunch.

Discussion Questions

1. What are some of the biggest temptations you face?

2. If you were to hang out with some of your "worst" friends, who would influence whom?

3. Who are students in your school that could sure use a friend like you?

4. What are ideas you could give your church in reaching out to people where you live?

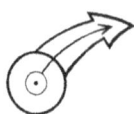

2.3 Connecting People With God

Q: My church seems to fight a lot about worship styles and what people should wear to church. Is there something bigger the church should be doing?

I am sorry that it seems that much of our church focus is on wrestling with worship styles and what we wear to worship God. The Church was created to be the voice, hands and feet of Jesus Christ. As the church, our job is to represent Christ in the world; that is what we "should be doing." It can be summed up in two easy statements: "Love God" and "Love Others."

Your question, it seems to me, is really, how do we as a church genuinely worship God, and how do we really love others?

What we call the "worship wars" have been going on for years, asking how we best worship God. Part of the reason this "fight" exists is that we all have different ways in which we seem to connect better with God. For the generation that grew up with hymns, that music helps them to connect better in worship. The present generation tends to connect better with God through band-oriented music. The danger for both is that we may start to worship "style" rather than God.

Some degree of learning and growing needs to happen in all of our lives. All generations have things to share and learn from each other.

What we wear can seem very trivial at first glance; however, there could be depth to it. For instance, when you are learning the game of football, you go over the basic rules of the game. When you truly understand the boundaries and guidelines of the game, they become natural for you (for instance, handling the ball, effective passing, rules of the pitch, etc.) Then you can work on plays and higher levels of learning.

Sometimes it seems that we make a big deal out of little things. The reality is, if we in the church were really solid in the basics of what the church should be doing, and how we should live our lives, then we can go on to other things. In some settings, people believe that we should give our best to God, so that is why we really dress up nicely. Other settings have a "come as you are" mentality because "it is all about the heart." We need balance of the two trains of thought.

Take a look at Acts 6:1-7. Disagreements in the early church had to do with the distribution of food and the need to preach and to teach. Some disciples were called to lead the worship, others to compassionate ministry. What was the big deal? Just this: that we need to maintain the purpose and importance of worship, how we minister, and how it represents Christ to our world.

Worship not only gives to God our attention and affection—which God enjoys—it is also done in a spirit of unity that strengthens our bond with fellow believers, which He also enjoys. It is a way in which we identify with both Christ and His church. It is through worship that God then provides each of us with the grace we need to sustain us in our Christian life. This grace empowers each of us to see the world as Christ sees it and to minister to it as Christ would minister to it.

Discussion Questions

1. In what style of worship service do you feel closest to God?

2. Do you remember a time when all generations came together and you saw the overpowering presence of the Holy Spirit?

3. In what setting do you worship? "Give God your best", or "come just as you are"?

4. Does what you wear to church distract others from worshipping God or cause people to focus on you?

2.4 Rules And Relationships

Q: My church seems to have a lot of rules. Is this really what Jesus intended when he created the church?

The essence of church is definitely not rules. However, it is important to understand that our God is a God of order. Spend time reading Leviticus and see how ordered God is. Read the Book of Numbers and you will find that God is very specific; He wanted to know exactly how many people were in each tribe.

I personally don't like the word "rules" when it comes to church. I relate better with the concept of "guidelines" or "boundaries" or "the sides of the road." In the game of football, could you image playing the game with no boundaries? What an interesting experience it would be for the players to start the game, and then watch as someone kicks the ball up into the stands and it lands right in a spectator's lap! All the players would come running up the stairs at the spectator, kicking at the ball. The people all around would get kicked because the players are going after the ball.

This would never happen because players know that they are to play within the boundaries of the pitch, and when the ball goes outside the boundaries, they stop because of the whistle and start over again. It is really fun to watch a great match that is played within the boundaries.

God has given us some boundaries for our lives, and part of the ministry of the church is to help us figure out what those boundaries in life are. New issues arise with each generation and each culture, and our challenge is to figure out how to live like Christ in this present age.

Jesus was asked, "What is the greatest commandment (Matthew 22:34-40)?" The expert in the law who asked Jesus this question didn't really want to know; it was just a test. The "law" was not given to us to become this list of rules to legalistically follow, but rather as a guide to help us know how to love God and how to love others.

Here is an example. When my wife was a child, her father gave the instruction to never leave sweets in her bedroom. The reason for this instruction was because they lived in an area where there were stinging ants that loved sweets. Well, my wife didn't listen and left a package of open chocolate in her bed. That night when she went to lie down and sleep, she wasn't alone in her bed! And before long she was covered with stinging ants and for days she carried the bite marks all over her body. This "rule" was given to protect Lori; it wasn't just a list of rules to follow.

If you feel like the church is just giving you a bunch of rules to follow, I would challenge you to take a look at your spiritual heart! Are you truly seeking God and wanting to become all that He intends for you? Have you been living outside of the boundaries that God has set for you and is He drawing some lines to help you see where you are?

I would challenge you to find someone in your church and talk about the things that seem like "rules" to you and ask, "Why is this a rule?"

Find out the reasons behind the guidelines and seek to understand them. I think you will find that you will appreciate the heart and spirit behind the rules.

Discussion Questions

1. What rules seem to irritate you the most?

2. Do you know why your church has this rule? (If not, find out!)

3. Have you given a rule or direction to someone else and they didn't respond well to you? Talk with a friend about how you felt.

chapter three

HOLINESS: THE QUALITIES OF A HOLY PERSON

by Clive Burrows

3.1 Seeking God With Everything

Q: So Jesus says the greatest commandment is to love God with our whole heart, mind, soul and body. How do I do that?

Jesus said this in answer to a Jewish religious teacher who asked Him which was the greatest commandment of all (Matthew 22:37, Mark 12:30, Luke 10:27). Although there were 613 recognized commandments at that time, Jesus did not pick any of them as the most important. Instead, he quoted one of the most known and memorized Old Testament passages:

"Attention, Israel! God, our God! God the one and only! Love God, your God, with your whole heart: love him with all that's in you, love him with all you've got!" (Deuteronomy 6:4-5, *The Message*)

Jesus shifted the focus from rules, laws and observances to relationship. Instead of merely giving us a "key commandment" to obey, Jesus invites us to respond to God with adoring love. Love is at the heart of relationship.

John describes how our amazing, unique, awesome God, who is absolutely holy, lavishes His love on us (1 John 3:1a), passionately and unconditionally. God's love is not a sentimental love but active and transforming and seeks our love in return. It is only when we accept or receive His "transforming love" that we can love Him in return (1 John 4:8b-10, 1 John 4:16b).

We can only love God with our whole heart, mind, soul and body when we allow His amazing, transforming love to flood our hearts and lives completely.

This is the work of God's Spirit, but requires our willingness to receive it and surrender to His Lordship. Another word for this is "consecration": giving all that I know of myself to all that I know of God. God does not hold anything back in His love for us and so He asks us to love Him without reserve, to love Him with everything we are and have and desire. He wants more than some parts of our lives. He seeks wholesome and holistic love, not compartmentalised love. When we allow Christ to be Lord in our lives then our self-centered love becomes God Christ-centered love.

Love God, your God, with your whole heart. Love him with all that is in you. Love him with all you have! When we do this, everything else, commandments, rules, etc., falls into place. In Luke's gospel Jesus goes further to add, "Love your neighbor as yourself." This is the extension of this relationship and love. When we receive God's amazing love and fully return that love, then we want to love others as we have been loved.

Discussion Questions

1. Jesus' words came from one of the most known scriptures of the Old Testament. What is more important than knowing things about God?

2. Why is a right relationship with God more important than codes of practice and keeping rules?

3. Why is it important to love God with more than just the spiritual part of our life?

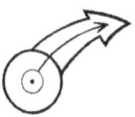

3.2 Seeking God As Yourself

Q: I have a lot of junk in my life that I know probably doesn't make God happy. But how can I clean those parts of my life up so that I can become a better Christian?

This is a great question because it recognizes that Christians often have "junk" or things in their life that sadden and disappoint God.

The starting point of the question, "how can I?" is the real issue. The truth is that we can't! The human tendency is to try to sort our lives out ourselves. Sometimes we can be partially successful in changing a few things, but those changes tend to be at the surface. It is impossible for us to clean up our act enough for us to make ourselves acceptable to God or make him happy. Instead, we are to give ourselves to God and let Him completely change and transform our life.

To deal with the real problem of junk in our lives we need God's help to deal with the deep issues that cause or allow the "junk" (or sin) in.

John puts it this way: "But if we walk in the light, as He is in the light, we have fellowship with one another, and the blood of Jesus, his Son, purifies us from all [every] sin. If we claim to be without sin, we deceive ourselves and the truth is not in us. If we confess our sins, he is faithful and just and will forgive us our sins and purify us from all unrighteousness" (1 John 1:7-9).

The first step is to acknowledge that we have junk (sin) in our life, even as a Christian, because when we acknowledge or confess it, we are also asking God to do something about it. We need to come to God just as we are—as ourselves. When we come to God in this honest attitude, acknowledging our sin, then God, who is merciful, loving and faithful, forgives our sin. This takes away the guilt and responsibility from us, while God's Spirit works at a deeper, transforming level to cleanse our lives of the deeper causes of the junk and sin, changing and purifying our deeper attitudes of self-centered, self-gratifying self interest or unrighteousness.

This changes not only our behavior (what happens at the surface level of life) but it changes our thinking, attitudes and disposition, what governs and determines who we are and what we do. We are no longer self-centered but Christ-centered and Christ is truly Lord of our life. But John also emphasizes that once this forgiveness and cleansing happen we need to live differently. "Walk in the light, as he is in the light… we have fellowship with one another, and the blood of Jesus, his Son, purifies us from all [every] sin."

So we need God's help not only to deal with the problem of sin and its cause. We need God's ongoing help to live Christ-centered, Christ-like lives! The Spirit of God then enables us to continue living a Christ-honoring life.

Paul also assures of this when he writes, "May God himself, the God who makes everything holy and whole, make you holy and whole, put you together - spirit, soul, and body - and keep you fit for the coming of our Master, Jesus Christ. The One who called you is completely dependable. If he said it, he'll do it!" (1 Thessalonians 5:23-24, *The Message*).

Discussion Questions

1. What kind of junk holds young people back from fully following Christ?

2. If Jesus accepts us just as we are, is it OK to remain the same and just keep asking Him to forgive us?

3. What is wrong with trying to sort out or straighten up our own lives before we follow Christ?

4. Why is it as important to continue to live a Christ-centered life as it is to receive forgiveness and cleansing from Him in the first place?

3.3 Seeking God in Different Ways

Q: I don't get a lot from reading the Bible and church makes me bored. Is there more to being a Christian then reading the Bible and going to church?

There is certainly a lot more to being a Christian than Bible reading and going to church: at the heart of being a Christian is a relationship with Christ.

When we get the relationship part right, then Bible reading and worship take on new meaning, new depths, new excitement. This relationship with Christ must be the priority. Paul explained His relationship with Christ in this way: "I consider everything a loss compared to the surpassing greatness of knowing Christ Jesus my Lord, for whose sake I have lost all things, that I may be found in Him…" (Philippians 3: 8).

Paul frequently speaks of the life of the Christian as the "in Christ" experience. He means that Christ should live fully in the life of the Christian and that Christians should live their lives in a completely Christ-centered way, becoming more and more Christlike in who they are, how they think and what they do.

The heart of the Good News is about our relationship to Jesus Christ, God's son. It is not, first of all, about church services and formal worship and the discipline of daily devotions but about a living, dynamic and growing relationship with God through His son by the power of the Holy Spirit.

When we settle the relationship issue, and this is the priority, then reading the Bible and being part of a worshipping church begin to take on new meaning, interest and excitement.

Bible reading is no longer a boring discipline; it becomes part of the desire to "know Christ" which Paul describes as "the surpassing greatness of knowing Him".

To have a real relationship with Christ we need to know Him. It is impossible to have a deep relationship with someone we only know at the surface level. Paul gave the first priority of His life to knowing Christ more and more—so should we.

But the Bible is not the only place where we meet Christ and get to know Him. We do this by living for Him, by following Him and obeying Him. We also learn to know Christ by worshipping together with others who have this same relationship with Him and are on the same journey because they are part of His family. Christ calls us into His family to be part of a worshipping community. Church is about meaningfully worshiping Christ together and listening to the voice of God's Spirit as we do. We not only learn on our own but we learn together as a community.

This doesn't mean that worship does not need to be relevant, meaningful and inspiring to all ages and all groups—it should! But we most help this by participating rather than merely being spectators. We must allow God's Spirit to minister to us through worship.

Discussion Questions

1. What do you think it means to "know Christ" and how can we make this a life-long pursuit?

2. What could you do to help worship to be more relevant and inspiring to you and your peers?

3. What are the biggest difficulties for you in reading the Bible and how could this be changed?

3.4 Seeking God During Hard Times

Q: My friend just died and God seems so far away. Is there something I can do to feel God's presence again?

Life's crushing experiences hit us at a deep emotional level and can anaesthetise our feelings or send them into angry turmoil and cause us to feel distanced from God. Our feelings can deceive us and convince us that God is absent, unconcerned, unable or unwilling to help. It is important to remember that it is quite normal to feel like this—it is often part of the process of grief.

In fact, everyone has times like this, of spiritual dryness or a lack of connection with the Lord Jesus. It can be caused by gradual sin that we've allowed into our life that creates a barrier between us and the Lord; or sometimes it's just a matter of fatigue. When emotions are confused, they can make us feel far away from God even though we may not be. It can also be caused by crisis like bereavement.

Emotions alone are never a valid measure of spirituality. It is wonderful to experience great emotional highs, but our relationship with Christ cannot be based on emotional signals or responses.

What do you do when God seems far, far away? When you try to read the Bible but it just seems like meaningless print? When you attempt to pray but just can't concentrate or connect and you feel like you're simply wasting your time? What do you do? How do you renew that intimacy with God?

Let's focus on one key issue: the route to intimacy with God is not based on knowledge, nor ritual nor trying harder, but on obedience. Jesus said in John 14:21, "Whoever has my commands and obeys them, he is the one who loves me. He who loves me will be loved by my Father, and I too will love him and show myself to him."

Obedience is the key to re-establishing intimacy with God. Notice what it says above: "he that loves me will keep my commandments." And then we receive the promise—Jesus and the Father will come and make themselves known and be real to us in response to our obedience.

When you are really low and feel distant from God, open the Bible and say to the Lord, "I don't feel much right now, but whatever I read I'll take seriously and search for a way to respond (obey) and put it into practice". Determine to obey anything you see in the passage. This will help to reset your spirituality and refocus in the right direction. There is no easy or instant formula, but when we start to focus on obedience, the intimacy and the accompanying emotions are often not far away.

Open your Bible, read a paragraph or two, and then in some specific way, respond to it. Love Him and love others. And I think you'll see that God will reveal Himself in a new way.

Discussion Questions

1. What does the story of the Storm on the Lake (Mark 4: 35–41) teach us about Jesus' love and concern for us in the difficult experiences of life?

2. Why is it dangerous to rely on feelings and emotions in understanding and experiencing God's presence?

3. Paul says that "faith" is the gift of God. It comes from God's generous love or grace. When our faith is limited, lacking and weak what can we do about it?

4. In any relationship there are quiet times. How should we cope when God seems silent?

chapter four

HOLINESS: SPIRITUAL DISCIPLINES

by Todd Waggoner

4.1 Scripture: Reading and Remembering

Q: I don't get a lot out of reading my Bible. Is there something wrong with the Bible, with me or with how I'm reading my Bible?

I'm going to guess the problem is with how you're reading your Bible. We believe the Bible to be the inspired word of God, good and beneficial for all Christians (2 Timothy 3:16). So the problem is not the Bible. That being said, you may want to see if another version or translation that is easier to read is available to you. The Bible also says that much of the Christian faith will appear as foolishness to non-believers (1 Corinthians 1:18). But the fact that you're asking such a question lets me know you are not the problem either. God says seek and you will find (Deuteronomy 4:29; Proverbs 8:17; Matthew 7:7) and you are clearly seeking. So let me help you figure out how you can improve your Bible reading skills.

The first thing to remember when reading your Bible is that, the more you read, the better it will be for you. When studying your Bible it's okay to focus on a chapter, verse or word, but when you want to read your Bible the goal should be to see how many chapters you can read in one sitting.

Another thing to remember when trying to read your Bible is to actually read your Bible. It's amazing how much time Christians spend reading books about their Bible, about how to read the Bible better, about how to be a better Christian or books of Christian fiction. Stop reading books about the Bible and just read your Bible. And don't give up if it is hard or feels unproductive. For many of us, reading is becoming a lost art. Often, reading seems awkward and difficult. Do not give up. The more you read, the more you will condition your mind to realize the impact of reading.

Here's another way to improve your reading habits: Most Christians read their Bibles when something is wrong in their life and they are looking to their Bibles for answers. A much more productive way to read your Bible is to read your Bible when times are good, then when a problem happens, return to passages you remember about characters that went through the same thing. For instance, if you are facing a time of temptation you could return to the stories of Joseph (Genesis 39) or David (2 Samuel 11). Facing a time of fear, turn to the stories of Daniel (chapter 6) or the Disciples

(Matthew 8). Facing a time of leadership, turn to the stories of Moses (Exodus 18) or Paul (Acts 15).

Finally, don't be afraid of the Old Testament. A lot of us find the Old Testament intimidating. The names, places and traditions seem old and we may feel we won't understand. However, the majority of the Old Testament is stories, and stories are universal. While we may not fully understand the customs or cultural differences of the characters, we can relate to their emotions. And the Old Testament characters feel a lot. They are scared, worried, ashamed, empowered, happy and confused. They laugh out loud with joy, cry out in pain and comfort their friends. These are things we can all relate to and these are the stories that enrich our lives and make reading the Bible so much fun.

Discussion Questions

1. What could I do to improve where and how I read my Bible?

2. Because of what I'm going through, what Bible character could I relate to right now?

3. How has God used the Bible to speak to me in the past?

4. How could I set aside more time in my day to read my Bible?

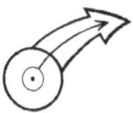

4.2 Prayer: Talking and Listening

Q: Christians talk a lot about prayer, but when I pray I don't hear anything. In fact, I feel like I'm talking to myself like a crazy person. Can I get some help?

Firstly, you need to know that you're not alone. Secondly, that doesn't mean that everything is okay. Being a Christian means having a relationship with God. And prayer is nothing more then talking and listening to God. Prayer is how we communicate, and communication is the most important thing to keeping a relationship alive and healthy. It is one of those things we cannot give up on. Below are a few obstacles that must be overcome.

The most common prayer that God answers in the Bible is a cry for help. Exodus begins with God saying, "I have heard my people cry out" (Exodus 3). A lot of the Psalms are nothing more then David crying out for help from his enemies (Psalm 17, 28, 55, 102, 143 and more). Jesus tells a story about sinner who cries out "have mercy on me God" and receives the mercy he was seeking (Luke 18). Too often we come before God with arrogance and command Him to do something for us or give us something we want. Prayer is about humbly coming with nothing before a God who is generous in His giving. If you want to see God answer your prayers stop telling Him what to do and simply cry out for help.

The second half of praying that many of us simply ignore is listening for God's answer. While God often comes in his might and power, like the whirlwind in Job 38, God just as often speaks with gentleness and compassion. Just like with Elijah, God comes to us as a silent breeze that whispers truth to our soul (1 Kings 19). We must learn how to be comfortable with silence and silent places if we ever hope to hear what God is saying. This is one of the reasons that morning devotional time makes so much sense for those of us that live in cities. We need to come to God before the hustle of crowds, the honking of car horns and the yelling of venders begins if we ever hope to hear God's whispers.

Another lesson to learn with prayer is that we need to be persistent. Jesus tells a story about a widow who comes before a judge every day asking for justice (Luke 18). Eventually, the judge realizes how important justice is for this widow who he had dismissed every day and grants her what she has been begging for. We too need to come before God this way, Jesus goes on to say. This seems to help us realize what is actually important to us. We think we want something, but if we're not willing to continue to pray for it, to really fight for it, to come before God and beg for it day after day, do we really want it? Does the parent whose child is sick and dying in the hospital just pray once to God for healing for their child? No, he or she prays non-stop, over and over again, asking for the same thing every minute of every day, waiting for God to move.

Another way to hear from God is to ask God for things He wants to give, not for things we want. If you want to hear God say yes, don't pray for the latest toy or gadget. Instead, ask God to use you. Come before God as an available servant looking for direction and you will hear God speak a lot sooner then you would have heard Him answer you about when you'll get the latest must have item you want.

Finally, it's possible that prayer feels uncomfortable to you because you're going through a period of spiritual dryness. It's normal for most Christians to go through a time in their lives when God doesn't seem as close as He used to. Prayers just don't get answered like they used to. The Bible just doesn't speak like it used to. This is normal, but doesn't mean you should give up until God seems close again. No, God will use these times to help us realize just how important He is to us. Keep up with your prayers, Bible reading and other spiritual disciplines. God will reward your faithfulness soon enough with his presence.

Discussion Questions

1. How much time a day do I spend talking to God?

2. How much time a day do I spend listening to God?

3. When I pray, do I spend more time telling God what I want or asking God to show me what He wants?

4. How can I create more quiet times in my day to listen to God better?

4.3 Groups: Confession and Connection

Q: I'm tired of Christianity that's all about "me and Jesus". What can we do as a church or youth group to grow in our faith?

Your desire to move from an individual faith to a group faith is a noble goal. The Bible is a "we story". In the Old Testament, God is interested in creating a nation of Israelites, not just a relationship with one Jew. And in the New Testament Jesus begins his ministry by choosing 12 followers (Mark 1). So it is good that you sense God pulling you into group faith. But I must warn you that it will not be easy. The more people there are, the more opinions there are. How you will resolve these differences will make all the difference. Here are some helpful tools.

The first thing that the group must be known for is love. Jesus says, "The world will know that you are my disciples by the way you love each other" (John 13:35). If the group cannot get along, if you cannot get along with the person you disagree with, then don't expect God to be glorified by the group. And if your church or youth group goals are not to bring glory to

God, then you need to rethink the goals. Love for others is our way to prove our love for God.

Read the New Testament letters for guidance. Paul, Peter, John and others wrote their letters to the early churches who were going through much that your group will go through. Issues of conflict, leadership, membership, group goals and much, much more are addressed in the New Testament letters. Keep an eye out for the phrase "one another". This is Paul's way of saying, "Make sure you do this." The list includes: greet one another (1 Corinthians 16:20), encourage one another (1 Thessalonians 5:11), educate one another (Romans 15:14), bear one another's burdens (Ephesians 4:2), love one another (1 Peter 1:22).

For your group to really succeed, you need to create one where grace and peace rule. Paul opens all 13 of his letters with these two words. Grace and peace will create a group where people of different opinions can co-exist. Grace and peace will create a group where new people feel accepted instead of judged. Grace and peace will create a group where big God-sized dreams have room to take root. Grace and peace will create groups where hearts are transformed. Grace and peace will create groups where forgiveness reigns over guilt. Grace and peace will create a group where members want to come back every week and new people will want to join.

Finally, and probably the hardest part to start doing, your group needs to create a time for confessions of faith and a time for confessions of wrongs. Confessions of faith, or testimonies, do two things. Firstly, they remind others that God is on the move, that God is moving in people's lives, that God is answering prayers, that God is still using His scriptures to speak new words. Secondly, confessions of faith provide truths that cannot be debated. Someone may disagree with what the pastor says in his or her sermon, but they cannot tell you that what you experienced never happened. Confessions of wrongs, or apologies, are also needed. Any time a group meets, people can get offended or hurt. When this happens, someone needs to say "I'm sorry" before the hurt turns into bitterness or anger. A place and time where people can say, "I've been hurt" and where others can say, "I'm sorry" will be a sign of grace and peace and where the anger will turn into love. And love is what brings glory to God.

Discussion Questions

1. What are some creative ways I can show grace, peace, love and support to others in my church or youth group?

2. Whom in my church or youth group do I need to forgive?

3. To whom in my church or youth group do I need to say I'm sorry?

4. What God-size dreams does God have for our church or youth group that I couldn't do myself but require everyone?

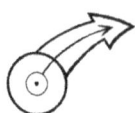

4.4 Stillness: Silence and Fasting

Q: I'm so busy in my life. Is there anything I can stop doing to strengthen my Christian walk?

The simple answer is: yes. From the very beginning (Genesis 2), God has called us to times of rest, times of quiet, times of Sabbath. So your desire to stop being so busy is a good and holy impulse. But even if you take a day of Sabbath every week, there are still times during the rest of the week that you may want to incorporate some spaces of quiet rest. Two of the ways Christians throughout history have stopped doing things in order to strengthen their faith have been using the spiritual disciplines of silence and fasting. Here are some insights to starting these two spiritual disciplines in your own life.

Know your motivation. If you are angry with your parents and choose not to talk to them, that is not the spiritual discipline of silence. Skipping a meal in order to lose a few pounds is a diet, not spiritual fasting. The purpose of all spiritual disciplines is to apply James 4:8 (Come near to God and God will come near to you) to our lives. If you take this seriously, several things will happen.

The first thing that will happen is that you will know God better. Psalm 46:10 says, "Be still and know that I am God." When we seek out silent places and become silent, God's whispering voice and the subtle nudging of the Spirit become easier to recognize.

Part of seeking out silence is becoming still. And when we are still we notice so much more. This is because meaning accrues with time. For example, if you go to an art museum and look at a painting for just a few seconds, you may notice the colors, shapes or characters in the painting. But if you stare at that same painting for a few minutes or hours you will begin to notice deeper truths. Truths such as the way the colors interact with one another, that the artist actually uses several shades of a color and not just one color, that the paint has a texture, that the artist put great details into the background that you had overlooked, the way the characters in the painting are interacting with each other. In the same way, when we become still we notice so much more about our surroundings. Part of being a mature Christian is simply being aware of where we are (Colossians 4:2) and asking the question "how could God use me here?"

A third lesson we learn by pursuing silence and fasting is just how self-centered we really are. When we fast a meal and feel hungry, it helps us remember all of those that will only eat one meal a day and the millions of less fortunate ones who go to bed hungry every day. By choosing to stop speaking, we find a connection to those who are handicapped and also cannot use one of their senses. All of a sudden, we become one with the blind, deaf, mute and lame.

If you are still having trouble creating a place of stillness, try getting out of the city (if you live in a city) or away from all the people in the village. When we surround ourselves with man-made buildings, man-made cars or other man-made things, or even lots of other people, it is easy to think about the greatness of mankind. But our goal is to think about the greatness of God (Deuteronomy 32:2, Luke 9:43). So go someplace where you are surrounded with what God created. Maybe God-made trees or other things that grow in nature where you live, God-made mountains, or maybe the ocean is nearer than even the next hill, and God-made animals. Get away from the televisions or radios, family drama or friends. Seek God all alone with stillness through silence and fasting and I'm sure you will find what you were looking for.

Discussion Questions

1. When was the last time I took a real Sabbath (day of rest) and was just still?

2. Where could I go to be surrounded by God's creation?

3. What might God show me if I took the time to really look at my neighborhood, school and church or youth group?

4. What things could I cut from my life and schedule to create moments of silence and fasting?

chapter five

MINISTRY: WHY WE DO MINISTRY

by Sabine Wielk and Tim Evans

5.1 God Wants It

Q: Does God care or want me to do anything about debt of poorer countries, the AIDS crisis, world hunger or extreme poverty?

Absolutely! He does! How can we love our neighbour–something Jesus said was essential (Matthew 22:37-40) without caring about these issues that shape the reality of our lives? We are all connected. And although "connected" looks different in every place, none of us lives in isolation. It may be the beggar on the street that you walk past every day who is asking you for a cup of water or some food. It could be the child on the street who could really use a clean shirt and trousers. Or it could be when you go shopping and check the labels of where things are produced. Sometimes it says it has been made in your own country, sometimes halfway around our big world. With that connection–whichever form that may take–simply seeing people on your way, through the Internet or through the news–it comes with a responsibility. You can pretend that the beggar is not there. But you will continue to see him.

You can pretend that the child does not need help, but when it looks at you asking for help, what do you answer? You can not pretend that everybody is happy. You cannot pretend that you could live your life without others around you, those who drive the buses you take, who cook the food you eat, who produce the things you buy. Do you care about them? Do we love these neighbours, whether they live within a few meters of our homes, or somewhere far away?

And what does it mean "to love"? The issues mentioned in the question seem overwhelming. Nobody on their own can solve the challenges that are described. So where do we start? Throughout the scriptures God has called his people to be a people who love mercy, act justly and walk humbly with him (Micah 6:8). Could that be a starting point? Look at Isaiah 1:16-17, Psalm 10, Matthew 5, Luke 4, 1 John 3:16. When you explore the gospels, what kind of God do you see? How does Jesus treat the people he meets? For whom does he care?

5.2 We're All God's Children

Q: I hear a lot of "saved versus unsaved" talk at my church, and people saying that we just need to get the unsaved to become more like us. Is making more of us the reason for doing ministry?

We need to remember that when we speak of saving people, we are speaking of healing, restoring and redeeming things that are broken. God is doing that. And very often, he chooses to do it through things that we do or say. "Making more of us" can never be the reason for ministry. Ministry comes out of loving God and people (see 5.1) and that leads to people asking why we do what we do, or why we are the way we are. If our lives reflect the love of God then often others will be compelled to follow Him.

Imagine that following Christ is the best thing that has ever happened to you. Would you not want others to know about it? Would you not want the people around you to know about Christ as well? It may be helpful to look at salvation and redemption as an ongoing process. Yes, we are restored in and through Christ Jesus. But living on this earth, every day we experience the hurt of broken relationships, the challenges of school or work, our need to love and be loved more and more. So every day we look to God for restoration and healing. And every day our desire to love more will inspire and encourage us to show this love to the people around us. And that will bring healing and restoration to those people around us.

If you read the stories in the gospels and in the book of Acts, can you find what motivated Jesus to minister to the people around him? Did he do it to have a lot of people follow him? Have a look at Luke 5:15-16.

And what motivated people to tell others about Jesus? Was it simply to be able to say there were more people in the "following Jesus" group? Or was it because they had found something that had transformed their lives, that had saved them, and that they wanted everybody to know about (like the woman in John 4)?

5.3 God Is Leading The Way

Q: I sometimes get the impression that I'm doing a lot of things for God as if God was taking some time off. Where is God when I, the youth group or the church is doing ministry?

There's a statue of Jesus in a church in Soweto, South Africa. Some gunmen came in during the apartheid years and grabbed the priest, dragged him to the statue of Jesus and then made him watch as they shot off the hands of the statue. So now, there is this statue with the arms still reaching out, but there are no hands. You can find photos of it on the Internet (look for Regina Mundi, the name of the church).

The statue without hands is a good image of Jesus, of God and the way he chooses to work through us. We are his hands and his feet. So yes, when we as a youth group, as a church or as individuals "do ministry" it could look like we are doing it for God and he's taking time off.

Is that true though? Imagine God is right there with you all the time. Imagine He's that friend of yours, who is with you as you dig your hands into the dirt and clean up the garden of your elderly neighbour. Or that He works next to you as you paint that wall in a school, or is coming with you as you visit someone in the hospital? When Jesus went back to heaven, He told the disciples that He would send them the Holy Spirit to have the strength to be his witnesses (check Acts chapter 1 for more of the story). And that's what he did. We are called to live our lives in communion with Christ. His Holy Spirit is at work in us and gives us the strength to serve him. So how about starting to look for him being at work in that old lady at church who brings the flowers so the place looks nice? Or how about in the child who dances when she sings?

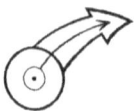

5.4 We Are All God's Priests

Q: I think I have some good ideas for helping others, but I'm not the pastor, youth pastor or even a youth leader. Should I just let them do their jobs?

Can anyone find a passage of the Bible that talks about the leader doing everything in the church? The role of a leader is never to do everything. The church is only alive when it operates as a collective. It is a body of believers called to be ONE who minister together (Ephesians 4:1-6).

Never be afraid to help others or to share ideas with leaders. What does Paul say about the body of believers in 1 Corinthians 12? Each believer has a part to play.

The root of what it means to minister is to "tend to the needs" of people: to be active in the healing of and caring for people who are in need. We believe in the God who came not to be served, but to live a life of service for others (Matthew 20:25 until the end of the chapter). The Christian life is shaped by love for one another and love for God. Therefore, all ministry finds its root in the calling to love God and love one another.

We "do ministry" because we are to be a people shaped in the likeness of Christ who emptied Himself for the interests and needs of others (Philippians 2:4-11). As such people, we treat those around us as he would have, with loving respect and care. When the church lives in this way, it points to the reality of God and his love for the world.

The apostle Paul uses the image of a body in 1 Corinthians 12 to describe how everybody who is a follower of Jesus is important and gifted. He insists that every part of the body, therefore every one of us, is important and that there is no "unnecessary" part who could just sit back and watch. And when he writes to Timothy in 1 Timothy 4, he encourages his friend to have confidence and to be an example to the other believers.

So it is twofold—we have no excuse to "just let them do their jobs" because it is just as much our responsibility to serve God, to serve other people, to share the ideas we have and to find ways to put the ideas into practice. We do not need a job or a title to do that. But at the same time, we should do it well, in a way that is an example—and also an inspiration—to others. That way, they will begin to share your ideas and help you to find ways to minister using your gifts.

So who are the people around you who could help you turn your ideas into reality? Hopefully those listed in the question who have the "job" will partner with you and support you. And you might be surprised who else has similar ideas that you could develop together with them. And how could your ideas, put into practice, serve others and through that serve God? What motivates you? Are your ideas, turned into action, building God's kingdom? Are you actively involved in sharing his love with the people you are in contact with?

chapter six

MINISTRY: TO WHOM WE MINISTER

6.1 To The Lost

6.2 To The Least Of These

6.3 To Each Other

6.4 To the Earth

by Kyle Himmelwright

6.1 To The Lost

Q: Jesus says He came to seek and to save. I want to follow in Jesus' steps, so how can I do this too?

Jesus did indeed come to "seek and save" the lost. By the power of His Holy Spirit, God graciously seeks out people to have a relationship with them, even before they realize He is seeking them. When they decide to give their lives to God, it is also God who saves them. We do not have to "seek and save" in this manner. What we have to do is to walk daily in a Christlike manner, so that when people see us, they get an accurate representation of who Jesus really is. If you are saying, "I want to follow in Jesus' steps," you have already begun to do so.

The journey of following in the steps of Jesus begins with the recognition that Christ, as the Son of God, is worth following! However, simply wanting to follow Christ is not enough. We must first understand who Jesus was on Earth and why He left His footsteps where He did. Read one of the first three books of the New Testament. Where did Jesus leave His footsteps? With whom did Jesus decide to walk? When we answer these questions, we will better understand where and with whom we need to be walking.

Discussion Questions

1. Why has God placed you where you are? With whom do you associate?

2. How can you creatively show Christlike love to the people in your life?

3. Have you ever looked at someone and thought they were made to do what they are doing? Why did you think that? What makes them a perfect fit for that ministry or job?

6.2 To The Least Of These

Q: I want to see my friends get saved but is evangelizing my friends the only kind of ministry I need to do?

Every person has a sphere of influence, a small corner of this very big world where what we say and do has an effect on people. To recognize that your friends need a relationship with Christ and that you can make a difference is a very profound realization. Also profound is the realization that our ministry is more than just evangelism. This is where the church comes into play. Paul, the very first missionary, compared the church of God to the human body. Every part must do its part in order for the body to function correctly. To find out what part of the body you are and what ministry He is calling you to, there are few helpful things you can do.

Firstly, you can pray about it. God has uniquely gifted you for a particular purpose. This purpose is not something He wants to keep hidden from you, but He wants you to seek it. When we pray, we seek and find the best that God has for us.

Secondly, think about how God has particularly gifted you. Do you make friends easily? Are you blessed with musical ability? Are you particularly successful in one area of life? If God has gifted you in a particular area, maybe He did so, so that you could offer that ability back to Him for His glory and service.

Next, ask people who know you what gifts for ministry they see in you. Often, we fail to see our own gifts because we assume that is just the way we are. Other times, we tend to be hyper-critical, unwilling to give ourselves a bit of credit for those things God has enabled us to do well.

Finally, volunteer with several different ministries to find out what passions God has placed within your heart. Often times, we do not realize how amazing an opportunity for service can be until we actually get involved and experience it firsthand.

When we seek God's will through prayer, reflecting on our particular gifts, conversations with others and firsthand experience, He gives us clarity.

Discussion Questions

1. Who are the "least of these?"

2. How many of the "least of these" do you have regular contact with?

3. What are some gifts you have already realized that you possess?

4. How can you use your gifts to perform a part of the body's (church's) responsibilities?

6.3 To Each Other

Q: I often think that Christians are not very nice to each other and should treat each other better. Does the Bible have anything to say about this?

You can tell an Italian by his or her language. You can tell a police officer by his or her uniform. You can tell a child by his or her size, and John 13:34-35 says that you can tell a Jesus-follower by his or her love. As Christians, we are called to a love beyond our immediate families and friends. During His mountaintop sermon in Matthew 5, Christ challenged His listeners to love even those who hate them.

The Bible is a large book, but Christ said it can really be summarized in two key ideas: love God with all that we are and love the people we come into contact with as much as we love ourselves. God is love (1John 4:8) and He demonstrated that by giving His Son to die for us even while we were right in the middle of sinning against Him (Romans 5:8)! If the very essence of God is love, can we truly bear the name "Christian" if we are unable to love those for whom Christ died?

Discussion Questions

1. What is absolutely essential to reaching our world for Christ?

2. In reaching people, what part does a building play? What about a Bible? An ordained pastor? Music? A denomination? Money?

3. How much of the fighting in the church is centered on non-essential issues?

4. What does Matthew 18:21-35 teach us about forgiveness?

6.4 To the Earth

Q: I feel closer to God when I'm outside in nature, but does God care about things like the environment and the extinction of animals?

The first chapter in the Bible tells us that upon the completion of His creative work, God took a step back, analyzed the results, and called it "good." From the sky, land and waters that God separated into their rightful places to the animals that walked, swam and flew, God was happy with what He had done. And with Adam and Eve, God was very happy. In His infinite wisdom, God created a balance of existence where the animals who could not swim had land to walk on which was filled with food sufficient for maintaining life. The fish had the water, and for the birds He created the air. There were billions of organisms and they were intricately pieced together in a masterpiece only God the Creator could have made. Chapter one of Genesis records God giving Adam and Eve one, and only one, bit of instruction: care for His creation.

Every time humans eliminate a natural habitat in order to build the next highway or shopping mall, we upset the delicate balance and the natural order of the Creator's masterpiece. When we choose to use and discard rather than recycle, when we prefer convenience over sustainability and when we consume faster than the creation can reproduce, we distort God's creation as surely as if we painted an X in the middle of Leonardo da Vinci's masterpiece, "Mona Lisa."

Just as a great painter signs his masterpiece, "the heavens tell of the glory of God, the skies display His marvelous craftsmanship" (Psalm 19). In other words, we know something about God because we have seen His work.

Paul understood that creation is actually an unspoken testimony about God. He wrote, "From the time the world was created, people have seen the earth and the sky and all that God made. They can clearly see His invisible qualities - His eternal power and divine nature. So they have no excuse whatsoever for not knowing God" (Romans 1:20). When we fail to care for His creation, we're not only showing disrespect for His creative nature, we're actually distorting His own personal revelation.

Discussion Questions

1. If God were to take a step back and re-analyze His creation, would He call it good?

2. When we look at God's creation, where can we see God?

3. Read Matthew 10:29. What does this verse tell us about how much God cares for His creation?

4. Read Colossians 1:19-20. Is Christ only planning to reconcile human kind to Himself or is His reconciliation more inclusive?

www.ingramcontent.com/pod-product-compliance
Lightning Source LLC
Chambersburg PA
CBHW020442030426
42337CB00014B/1354